Contents

THE RAMBLERS' ASSOCIATION promotes country walking, protects rights of way, campaigns for access to open country, woodlands, etc. and defends the beauty of the landscape. The RA plays a major role in securing legislation to protect our paths and countryside. Please give your support by becoming a member. Write to:
The Ramblers' Association, 1/5 Wandsworth Road, London SW8 2XX. Tel: 0171 339 8500

BERKSHIRE AREA
The RA has seven Groups across the County. Each arranges its own extensive programme of walks and endeavours to monitor the local footpaths, to seek improvements and oppose any threats. For details contact: Mr John Moules, 50 Qualitas, Roman Hill, Bracknell, Berks. RG12 7QG.

* *At time of publication the route we describe here, although freely available for public use, may not be the correct (legally defined) right-of-way. We have asked the Highway Authorities to give priority attention to resolving all these anomalies. Our map shows the definitive route.*

Windsor / Datchet Circular

A Right Royal Romp of a walk as we encircle Queen Victoria's Home Park, using newly created sections of the Thames Path National Trail.

Distance: 8½ (level) miles
Maps: OS Pathfinder 1173 Windsor;
East Berks RA Group's
'Windsor & the Great Park'
footpath map
START/FINISH: Windsor's Central
Station (Thames Trains)

From Central Station walk up slope and turn left down Thames Street. Keeping Castle on right, continue past Theatre Royal and round the corner. Cross at traffic lights into pedestrianised roadway.

With Windsor Bridge (some call it Eton!) ahead, turn right down steps into Thames Side and by 'Donkey House' enter Romney Walk. At end of railings bear left on roadway to boatyard by Romney Lock. Pass right of launching dock and through swing–gate ahead (after perhaps visiting the lock and Cobblers Path, an old path along the lock island).

Continue on riverside passing under Black Potts railway bridge and into Home Park with fine backdrop provided by the Castle, a unique setting for the annual Horse Show here in May. The public towpath stops at Victoria Bridge. Cross river here and from right–hand footway take steep steps down to the riverbank and along a new stretch provided for the Thames Path. After a distance, path leads to road at start of Datchet. Cross over, turning right, until at Queen's Road you can avoid the traffic for a short distance by using the strip of riverside gardens.

Today nothing remains of an old bridge built here in Queen Anne's time (1706) which carried a public road to Park Street, Windsor. By Act of Parliament in 1848 the old way was closed and two new bridges (which we use), named appropriately Victoria and Albert, were built either side of Datchet.

Rejoin footway fronting pretty Old Bridge House and after The Avenue,

choose an opportunity to cross onto the right–hand footway. Pass the ornate entrance to 'Poplars' and on verge ahead, just after 'Sandlea Court', turn right into newly created fenced Thames Path. Follow field edges back to the river and on to the Albert Bridge (1851, rebuilt 1928). Follow the path under, then over the bridge, to continue down–stream along the other bank. A weir marks the parting of the river from the New Cut (built 1822, creating Ham Island) as we follow bank ahead to Old Windsor Lock.

Just after lock, notice on far bank quaint thatched property, aptly named 'Honeypot Cottage', home for many years of actress Beryl Reid. Towpath soon crosses concrete bridge and within a few paces turn sharp right beside marina. At entrance gate to moorings turn left up enclosed path to 13th century church of St Peter & St Andrew, Old Windsor. One Mary Robinson is buried here; a talented actress and beauty known as 'Perdita' – the Fair Shepherdess, seduced by the Prince of Wales, later George IV. Her tomb lies north of the church.

The Long Wall

Leave by lych gate and follow road ahead and where this bends right, go straight on, to left of houses. Path narrows at metal barrier. At road turn left, then second right – Follett Close – and pass right of No. 9 to emerge in service road beside A308 Straight Road. Carefully cross main road via traffic

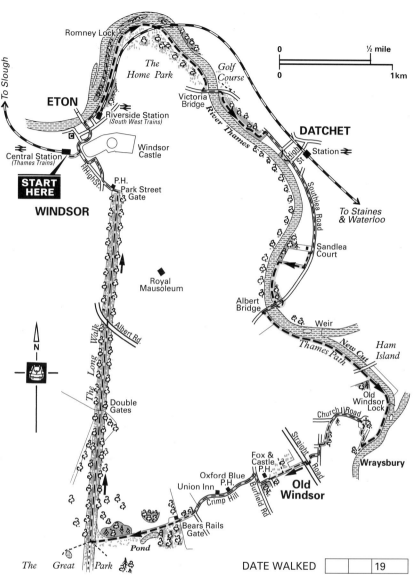

START HERE

WINDSOR

ETON

To Slough

To Staines & Waterloo

DATCHET

Romney Lock

The Home Park

Golf Course

Victoria Bridge

River Thames

Riverside Station
(South West Trains)

Central Station
(Thames Trains)

Windsor Castle

High St.

High St.

Station

Southlea Road

P.H.
Park Street Gate

Royal Mausoleum

Albert Rd.

The Long Walk

Double Gates

Sandlea Court

Albert Bridge

Weir

New Cut

Thames Path

Ham Island

Old Windsor Lock

Church Road

Straight Road

Wraysbury

Fox & Castle P.H.

Oxford Blue P.H.

Union Inn

Crimp Hill

Burfield Rd.

Old Windsor

Bears Rails Gate

Pond

The   Great   Park

N

DATE WALKED

		19

sland, pass through metal swing–gate nd straight ahead alongside recreation rea. Pass 'Fox & Castle' and turn right long road, then cross over into Crimp Hill. Where this road bends after school, o straight ahead to Bears Rails Gate of Windsor Great Park.

n Park keep straight ahead to gate in deer fence, following hedge on right. Well defined path passes right of tree ringed Prince of Wales Pond, hen left of fenced copse. View across pen parkland the majestic Copper

Horse (George III) on Snow Hill. Soon turn right to follow Long Walk two miles to the Castle; this magnificent double row of London plane trees and horse chestnuts was originally planted, with elms, in 1696. In front of Castle gates turn left into Park Street. *At this point allow 10 minutes to reach Central Station.*

At road junction fork right (signed 'Castle Entrance'). At end of St Alban's Street turn down past Henry VIII's Gateway (public exit from Castle) to return to station beside 'Ye Harte & Garter'.

Maidenhead to Windsor Ramble 2

Step this way for a great escape (from a town), have a brief encounter (with an unspoilt village), reflect on the future (rowing lake) and reach a historic climax (the largest inhabited castle in the world)!

Distance: 7¼ miles
OS Maps: Explorer 3 Chiltern Hills South;
          Pathfinder 1173 Windsor
START: Maidenhead Station
FINISH: Windsor Central Station

From station main entrance walk down left side of forecourt, use pedestrian crossings over roadways ahead and turn right. Go under railway bridge and immediately turn left on footway which skirts right of striking multi–storey car park. At road ahead (Staverton Way) turn left past Royal Mail depot. Shortly cross over and turn right on tarmac path signed 'Green Way'.

At T–junction turn right on roadway soon dwindling to track. After metal gate go straight on with high bank on left. Where minor paths branch off both sides, turn left up slope bearing right and follow feint grass path along crest of high ground (Braywick Park). Path leads down through gap in fences and shallow steps. Turn right to cross footbridge and at meeting of paths turn left along drive to road. Carefully cross over turning right, then shortly left (still 'Green Way')

by group of pretty Victorian cottages. Pass between white rails into treelined Causeway which crosses stream (The Cut) and leads to Bray village.

Turn right for a few yards along High Street, then cross into entrance drive of 14th century St Michael's Church, whose turncoat vicar is recalled in the well known lines:

> *And this is law, I will maintain*
> *Until my dying day, Sir,*
> *That whatsoever King may reign,*
> *I'll still be the Vicar of Bray, Sir.*

Pass to right of church and leave graveyard in far right corner. Emerging at road (Ferry Road) turn left to view famous Thames–side restaurant, The Waterside Inn, (one of only four in the UK with 3 star Michelin rating). Retrace steps from slipway and turn left in front of black and white terrace, Bettoney Vere, leading to Old Mill Lane. After the 'Fish' use the tree lined roadside path, becoming Monkey Island Lane. Cross motorway bridge and continue along road; where this turns left go ahead on drive until gravel conveyor is reached. Here turn left over The Cut and cross the Thames by new 'conveyor bridge', built to transport part of the 4½ million tons of gravel to create Eton College's new 2 km. long rowing lake. Due for completion in 2007, costing over £10 million, the facility will include a nature reserve and arboretum.

On far side of river, turn downstream for about 100 yards then left, along hedgerow. Follow new waymarked path,

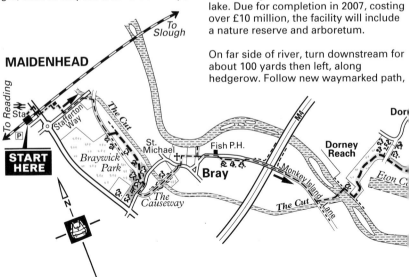

over footbridge. At a future date our route will go straight over the site access road ahead but meanwhile we must follow path beside road, then back on the other side.

This new winding bridleway leads finally to edge of the unenclosed Dorney Common. At stile ahead, turn left through gate and head across Common towards left end of row of trees. Cross road to stile in angle of these trees and at end of broad strip between fields (Roasthill Lane), turn right on field headland, then left down chestnut tree lined drive to reach river by Boveney Lock.

Go downstream until immediately after footbridge (Boveney Ditch); here turn left for a few paces, then take the farthest right mid–field way. Keep right when joining permanent bridleway and stay on this track towards archways (of A355) in distance, with pinnacles of Eton College

chapel beyond. After tunnel, continue about half–way along field side and fork right, aiming for 7th arch of rail viaduct. (The line opened in 1849, the viaduct being rebuilt of brick in 1865. To discourage ideas of truancy, Eton College erected a 10ft high wall!)

On far side of arch keep straight on over grass towards cluster of tall chestnut trees. Path ahead crosses two playing fields, with road between; then goes straight on through car park, to reach road leading into High Street, Eton. Here turn right over river–bridge and go straight ahead at traffic lights up Thames Street, opposite castle walls, to find Central Station on right, almost at top of hill.

DATE WALKED   19

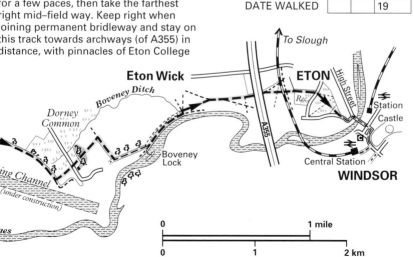

Slough to Cookham

Take a fine Spring or Autumn day, stir in the beautiful colours of Burnham Beeches, add a handful of great poetry, and a pinch of the Thames – and what have you got? A feast of a walk!

Distance: 10 miles
OS Map: Explorer 3
                   Chiltern Hills South
START: Slough Station
FINISH: Cookham Station

From exit at Platform 5 walk up Railway Terrace and turn right along Stoke Road. Not exactly salubrious but think positive; this is the way *out* of Slough. 20 minutes walking brings us to the cemetery. For most of us the end but today it's really the beginning!

Beyond the Crematorium, by Stoke Place Farm, cross road and follow tree–lined cinder path. Shortly turn right beside driving range, go straight on between pines, then beside long wall. Cross one road and continue between playing fields, then another road to enter Gray's Field (NT) with memorial of 1799 to Thomas Gray (1716–1771). His much–loved 'Elegy written in a Country Churchyard' brings visitors from all corners to the nearby Church of St Giles and adjacent gardens.

Continue over Gray's Field to opposite corner and cross road. Now count the fields and in the second of these path goes through gap in hedge. At start of fifth field, take left of two paths, pass between garden and vegetable plot to road. Turn left for 20 paces, then left again, going diagonally half–right across field. On far side, at gap in boarded fence, stay on same line for 35 paces, turn 90 degrees right, (for definitive path see detailed map inset), then steer a straight course to road exit by The Nonsense House.

Turn right for 40 yards then sharp left. Small concrete footbridge points the line (waymarked trees) across the course (Farnham Park). On far side exit through swing–gate hidden in trees. At end of enclosed path cross into furthest of two roads, pass Kemsley Chase and shortly turn into Purton Lane. After Purton Court take footpath on left which leads to Farnham Common, opposite 'Green Man'. Turn right up main road (A355), crossing over to bear left into old road and enter footpath on left by barrier. Two lengths of enclosed path with road between brings us out facing the famous woodland known as Burnham Beeches (600 acres bought by the City of London Corporation in 1880 and maintained since then as a public open space).

Part of Hartley Court Moat

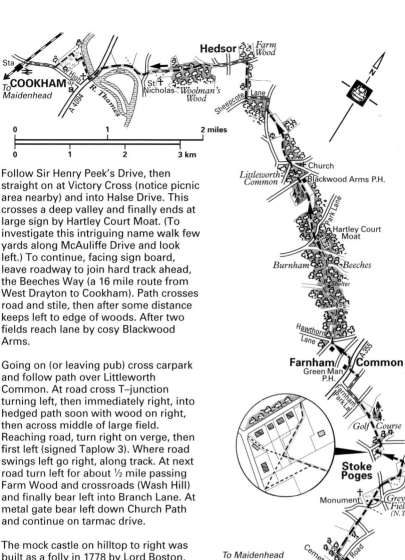

Follow Sir Henry Peek's Drive, then straight on at Victory Cross (notice picnic area nearby) and into Halse Drive. This crosses a deep valley and finally ends at large sign by Hartley Court Moat. (To investigate this intriguing name walk few yards along McAuliffe Drive and look left.) To continue, facing sign board, leave roadway to join hard track ahead, the Beeches Way (a 16 mile route from West Drayton to Cookham). Path crosses road and stile, then after some distance keeps left to edge of woods. After two fields reach lane by cosy Blackwood Arms.

Going on (or leaving pub) cross carpark and follow path over Littleworth Common. At road cross T–junction turning left, then immediately right, into hedged path soon with wood on right, then across middle of large field. Reaching road, turn right on verge, then first left (signed Taplow 3). Where road swings left go right, along track. At next road turn left for about ½ mile passing Farm Wood and crossroads (Wash Hill) and finally bear left into Branch Lane. At metal gate bear left down Church Path and continue on tarmac drive.

The mock castle on hilltop to right was built as a folly in 1778 by Lord Boston, an equerry to George III. (A short detour to left leads to St Nicholas Church, Hedsor, offering fine panoramic views.) At end of drive, cross road, enter green swing–gate and shortly turn right skirting large house (Hedsor Wharf). From footbridge keep left and after second stile head straight over field to stile at left end of roadside hedge. Turn left, crossing over, and on far side of Cookham Bridge turn right down steps. *From here allow 30 minutes to reach station.*

Now follow riverbank until at Marsh Meadow turn left beside sailing club. At back of enclosure turn right across field and on far side left, on well defined grass path leading to car park on Cookham Moor (NT). Cross road ahead and turn right on old causeway. Rejoin road, pass Spencer's, and continue until reaching shops and Cookham Station.

DATE WALKED | | 19

Taplow/Hitcham Circular

Walk this way for a brush with history. Follow the chain of old stile–free Ways, old woods, old manors, leading to the splendid burial mound of a Saxon warrior.

Distance: 5 miles
OS Map: Explorer 3 Chiltern Hills South
START/FINISH: Taplow Station

With your back to main station buildings, turn right down Approach Road and left along footway (Station Road). Some 50 yards beyond first lamp standard on *right* of road, cross shallow ditch on left and continue, now on tree-lined bank.

Rejoining footway, at road junction ahead cross over, turning left, along wide verge of Boundary Road. At end of field hedge on right, turn right along one of many old surfaced field paths in this parish. Look right along here over Poplar Farm fields for view of Windsor Castle on skyline. At road turn left to junction of Hitcham Road and Lane (the high wall conceals grounds of Victorian Hitcham House). A few yards to right stands the 12th century St Mary's Church. In the chancel is a brass to Nicholas Clarke in armour, who died 'of the swett' in 1551.

To continue, from road junction head north on bridleway (can be muddy), soon providing glimpses of historic

Hitcham Park on right. On the 2nd October 1602 Queen Elizabeth I visited Sir William Clarke, son of the above mentioned gent, whose house stood in this park. Sir William 'so behaved himself that he pleased nobody, and gave occasion to have his misery and vanity spread far and wide.'

Our path turns right and shortly enters woodland, turning left between the first two of many magnificent sweet chestnuts. Continue on this line, crossing new golf club drive (remembering Mark Twain's quip: "Golf – a good walk spoilt."). Just before road ahead turn left along recently created Permitted Path through wooded fringe of Hunt's Wood. At T-junction in far corner of wood turn left and enjoy the wide, sometimes banked, wooded wonderland of Hunt's Lane, leading us past 3 storeyed Hitchambury Manor.

At road cross over, turning left along narrow verge, then right, into Buffins. Where road bends take diagonal footpath across green and then beside vineyard. At T–junction turn sharp right along narrow fenced path leading to road. With care cross road (it's safer to walk a few yards left before doing so), then straight ahead through side entrance of Taplow Court. This short public path leads to old churchyard

The authors on the Saxon Mound at Taplow Court

beside 7th century burial mound of Saxon chief Taeppa, from whose name Taplow is derived. The mound was excavated in 1883 revealing swords, shields, gold ornaments, even a lyre, all now in the British Museum. Taplow Court and grounds are usually open on Sundays from Easter until end of July. For details tel: 01628 773163.

Return to the roadside, turn right down hill and first left along footway of Rectory Road to reach in a few minutes Taplow's pretty village green. *From here allow 30 minutes to reach station.* Go past 'Oak & Saw' and opposite end of green turn right beside St Nicholas House. After swing–gate into field carefully follow

remaining tarmac path over middle of two fields, as it zig–zags (two zigs and one zag!) to emerge at final roadside swing–gate. Here turn left down to main road (A4) and left again past the 'Dumb Bell' until, in front of railway bridge, take left fork to return to station.

DATE WALKED ☐☐ 19

River Thames

Hunt's Wood

Golf Course

Taplow Common Road

Hitchambury Manor

Hunt's La.

Hill Farm Road

Baffins

Hitcham Park

St Mary

Hitcham Lane

Taplow Court

Mound

Rectory Rd

Oak & Saw P.H.

TAPLOW

Boundary

Poplar Farm

Berry Hill Farm

Berry Hill

Road

Station Road

START HERE

MAIDENHEAD

Bath

Dumb Bell P.H.

Approach Road

Taplow Station

To Slough

To Maidenhead

A4

To Slough

| 0 | | 1 mile |
| 0 | | 1 km |

Furze Platt to Bourne End

Furze Platt may not resemble the Garden of Eden but the first ten minutes of this walk is a small price to pay for the delights to come; the pastoral peace of Widbrook Common and the matchless sweep of ancient meadow at Cock Marsh.

Distance: 4½ miles
OS Map: Explorer 3 Chiltern Hills South
START: Furze Platt Station
FINISH: Bourne End Station

Leaving platform at station turn left over level crossing and join left–hand footway (Harrow Lane). At 'Farmer's Boy', use traffic island to cross (Cookham Road) and turn left, then shortly right, into Moorside Close, signed to Green Way. Go straight on into footpath on left of playing field, cross road, then along short stretch of fenced path leading to open space (North Town Moor NT). The Moor was purchased by Maidenhead Corporation in 1928 from the Lord of the Manor of Cookham and remains a very pleasant public open space.

Go straight across Moor and through swing gate in far corner, then fork left to footbridge (over prosaically named Maidenhead Ditch). Here Green Way splits and we follow the East arm over uncultivated moor. On far side go through gap in hedge and head along mid–field path leading to remains of metal stile. Leave field and go straight ahead along gravel farm track. The tree clad ridge on the horizon stretches from the chateau style roofs of Taplow Court half–right, to the stately pile of Cliveden (NT) half–left. Just before metal field gates ahead, turn left on mid–field path. The hedgerow in front forms part of Maidenhead Borough boundary. Notice by stile one of the original boundary stones, engraved 'MB', which cost the equivalent of 37.5p when purchased in 1934.

Beyond stile the banks of White Brook with Widbrook Common (NT) ahead may suggest a picnic. Under supervision of the Hayward, commoners still graze their cattle here from mid–May to mid–November, the rent going to Cookham Educational Charity, set up in the past for apprentice boys. Over the wooden bridge the path divides. Keep straight ahead to cross stile in far left field corner, then walk beside old metal fence and cross footbridge (Strand Water). Shortly, just before concrete bridge, turn sharp right over stile and along left side of field, followed by paddock, to stile on far side. Cross track and now keep going straight ahead on path, sometimes fenced, following a variety of stiles, finally to reach road at edge of Cookham Moor (NT).

Widbrook Common and Cliveden

Returning from Bourne End

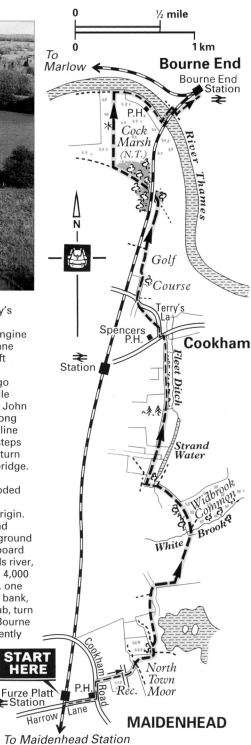

Here turn left, then right, into Terry's Lane. On the corner, opposite Old Farmhouse, notice one–time fire engine station with its flaming weather vane aloft. After about 100 yards fork left beside 'Tremayne'. Rejoining lane continue for some 40 yards, then go half–right up track to enter over stile Winter Hill Golf Course (owned by John Lewis Partnership). Follow path along edge of course, soon with railway line nearby. At bottom of slope a few steps leads down to path junction. Here turn left, go over stile and then under bridge.

The path ahead, terraced with wooded slopes towards the Thames, is an ancient track, perhaps of Roman origin. Cock Marsh has been common land since at least 1272. Reaching level ground turn right along a raised wooden board walk and then head straight towards river, passing to side of hillock, in fact, a 4,000 year old Bronze age burial mound, one of four hereabouts. Reaching river bank, opposite Upper Thames Sailing Club, turn right and follow towpath as far as Bourne End railway bridge (1895). The recently added walkway allows us to cross river. On far side go under the bridge then sharp left up a few steps and along path through car park to Bourne End Station.

DATE WALKED

		19

Maidenhead Thicket to Cliveden Reach

This is almost a National Trust Trail; across the broad acres of Pinkneys Green to a newly created nature reserve, a length of Cookham Moor and finally along the superb Hanging Woods of Cliveden.

Distance: 7½ miles
OS Map: Explorer 3 Chiltern Hills South
START: Bus stop on A4, town–side of Maidenhead Thicket, or car park just north of A4 roundabout. Both grid ref: 860 808.
FINISH: Maidenhead Bridge

From bus stop walk to roundabout and turn right onto footpath along the right–hand side of this fine NT open space. From car park walk past footbridge and turn left to cross road, then head across open space, bearing left along edge of common with woodland on right.

Stay close to woodland where it bears right, cross metal track and go straight on, tree lined at first, then over open green to cross road (Pinkneys Drive), bearing left into Lee Lane by 'Stag & Hounds'. Some 60 yards beyond the pub, cross over road and maintain same direction along the right–hand side of Pinkneys Green. This well preserved area forms part of 848 acres of Maidenhead and Cookham commons acquired in 1934 by public subscription and presented to the National Trust.

Where the right–hand hedge swings right keep straight on across open green. On reaching corner of copse ahead fork left. At group of (six) small trees turn right and head towards road. Cross carefully and after 25 yards turn left to follow line of trees. About 60 yards before end of common ('Robin Hood'PH) fork right along bridleway through woodland. Cross minor road and then bear away from houses to cross another lane (Winter Hill Road) to enter Malders Lane.

Opposite Kiln Place (more flint than brick!) notice new NT plaque –'Brick and Tile Works' which makes a delightful picnic stop, particularly if you can find the ponds! This site is being laid out by the Trust with emphasis on disabled access (notice tapping rails). Continuing along Malders Lane, keep left of red brick building at Hindhay Farm. About halfway along field on left,* turn left through gap in hedge and straight across field ahead to pass through neck of wood (Beeching Grove). At corner of wood, continue in same direction across middle of field towards distant buildings of Mount Farm. On far side turn right along wide grass headland, leading to Spring Lane.

Turn right down road (Long Lane) and look carefully for path opening in hedge of large field on left. Now follow diagonal line of this very old path (which originally continued directly to Cookham Moor) across two fields, through line of newly planted trees and over a gravel track. Path continues with fence on right to reach back of houses, passing between two similar terraces to reach estate road. Follow footway (Lesters Road), then cross road ahead and turn left along service road. Shortly turn right down Broom Hill and left at T–junction. Between nos. 49 and 61 turn into spur and head for gap into playing field. (Is *any* activity permitted here?)

Fortunately, there is nothing to stop us admiring the view towards Cliveden (NT and a many starred hotel). Ignore the definitive path which runs diagonally to left and instead head towards bungalow roofs visible over the brow of the slope. At the bottom of this slope exit from far left–hand corner of field into Shergold Way, leading to Peace Lane, soon to find the level crossing at Cookham Station.

Follow the main road until, just beyond a narrow stretch, cross over to continue in same direction on traffic–free old road over Cookham Moor. Unless visiting the centre of Cookham, in front of the war memorial turn right along School Lane and at the end cross Sutton Road into Mill Lane opposite.

At end of lane, at Mill House, turn right into hedged path soon becoming well defined woodland path leading to long-ceased My Lady Ferry. Now turn right

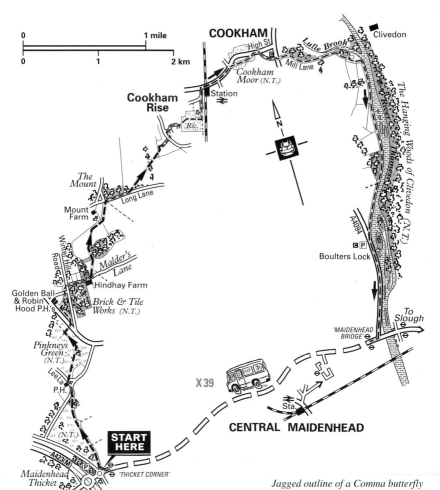

COOKHAM

High St

Lulle Brook

Clivedon

Mill Lane

Cookham Moor (N.T.)

Station

Cookham Rise

Rec.

The Mount

Long Lane

Mount Farm

Malder's Lane

Winter Hill Road

Hindhay Farm

Golden Ball & Robin Hood P.H.'s

Brick & Tile Works (N.T.)

Pinkneys Green (N.T.)

Leela P.H.

(N.T.)

START HERE

A423(M)

Maidenhead Thicket

To Reading

'THICKET CORNER'

The Hanging Woods of Clivedon (N.T.)

The Thames

A4094

Boulters Lock

To Slough

'MAIDENHEAD BRIDGE'

X 39

Sta.

CENTRAL MAIDENHEAD

0   1 mile
0   1   2 km

N

Jagged outline of a Comma butterfly at the National Trust's 'Brick & Tile Works'

along one of the most beautiful stretches of the River Thames – Cliveden Reach. Opposite the first small island, high up on the edge of Cliveden's Hanging Woods, a viewpoint commemorates Peter Nevell who originated this series of *Rambling for Pleasure* booklets over twenty years ago.

Follow the towpath for about 1½ miles to reach Boulter's Lock, the best–known lock on the river, immortalised in an Edwardian painting by E. J. Gregory called 'Boulter's Lock – Sunday Afternoon'.

At this point allow 15 minutes to reach the return bus stop on the A4 about 100 yards right of Maidenhead Bridge, shortly visible ahead.

DATE WALKED ☐ ☐ 19

Marlow to Bourne End

Small is beautiful! A short, level walk; through unchanging Thames water meadows with a backdrop of Chiltern hills and Berkshire beech woods.

Distance: 3¼ miles
OS Map: Explorer 3 Chiltern Hills South
START: Marlow Station
FINISH: Bourne End Station

Walk along Station Approach and in front of 'Marlow Donkey' turn left along Lock Road. At T–junction with Gossmore Lane cross ahead, turning right.

Our route out of Marlow lies along the tarmac path which bears left within a few yards. But first, we strongly recommend

Passing shadows at Marlow Lock

a short detour to view Marlow Lock and its delightful surroundings. For this, follow road ahead past tall white houses and find lock path on left.

This is a wonderful spot for watching river traffic and admiring views of the weir, All Saints Church and William Tierney Clark's elegant suspension bridge. Can you spot the sundial on Thames House? Notice cleverly rebuilt Mill House and its modern neighbours, the angular roofed clap boarded group designed by J. Seymour Harris.

To continue the walk, return along Gossmore Lane and turn right, signed Thames Path, to follow it downstream. Soon pass between some properties and river, then under bypass bridge. Good views ahead to Quarry Wood rising steeply from river on the Berkshire bank, followed by Winter Hill, a fine viewpoint. River bears left opposite the Scouts' national boating centre and we enter a poplar-lined public open space (Riverwood). A notice announces 'Westbury Farm' and we thread our way through swing–gates linking water meadows, with a fine sweep of Chiltern Hills away to left.

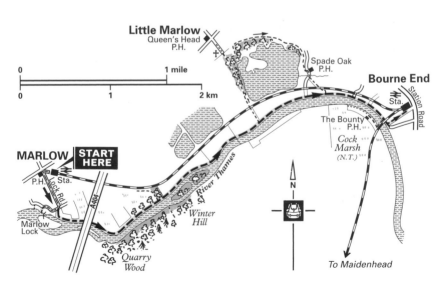

Enjoy the ride....the Thames near Spade Oak

Facing Spade Oak Meadow there is an option to lengthen route by a mile or so by turning away from the river and following a mainly lake side loop, visiting pretty Little Marlow (see map). Otherwise, stay along riverside to end of field (where road on left leads to Spade Oak pub).

Thames Path continues now on gravel drive, then through Upper Thames Sailing Club enclosure until, at end of boatyard, bear right to enter very narrow fenced path between house and river.

Keep straight on to pass under Bourne End railway bridge, then immediately turn left, up slope, leading to station. (Note: It may be useful to know that trains wait here for 5 minutes before reversing out. Once upon a time the line went on from here to High Wycombe and beyond.)

DATE WALKED [   ] [19]

RAMBLING ON....
East Berks Ramblers publish a number of guides in the 'Rambling for Pleasure' series, covering much of Berkshire and parts of adjacent counties. These are available in many local bookshops, libraries, information centres, etc. For a list/order form, send a SAE to East Berks RA Group, PO Box 1357, Maidenhead, SL6 7FP

Maidenhead Thicket to Henley

Climb the wooded slopes of Forestry Commission's Ashley Hill, admire the Chiltern Hills from across the Thames Valley; you might even spot a future Derby winner!

Distance: 8½ miles
OS Map: Explorer 3 Chiltern Hills South
START: Bus stop on A4, town–side of Maidenhead Thicket or car park just north of A4 roundabout. Both grid ref: 860 808.
FINISH: Bus stop east side of Henley bridge.

FROM BUS STOP walk to roundabout and turn right along left side of common. At first gap in trees turn left and cross road to car park.

FROM CAR PARK cross motorway footbridge and immediately turn right, along edge of Thicket (easy on the eye, 'orrible on the ear!). Continue parallel to motorway until way ahead forks. Here bear left along wide avenue of fine trees, passing Robin Hood's Arbour (NT – prehistoric Belgic farm enclosure). At end of avenue pass front of lodge (Stubbing's House –Queen Wilhelmina of the Netherlands lived here during WW2). Cross two drives and stiles into field and follow line of chestnuts.

Continue into field ahead now with hedge on left, leading to farm buildings at Burchett's Green. Turn left along road for some 80 yards then turn right, opposite Stubbing's Manor with its unusual 'dove tower'.

Gravel drive becomes narrow path through trees. At road by school car park cross over, turn right for a few yards before entering enclosed path to right of Burchetts Place. Follow right–hand side of fields to cross two stiles in copse before turning right along road. Just round bend in lane enter metalled footpath on left, rising continually to reach the highest point of our route, the 474 ft. high Ashley Hill.

Facing 'Clifton' (which has replaced a delightful Victorian forester's cottage), turn right. At bottom of hill cross track and go straight on. (Turn right for Dewdrop Inn nearby). Beyond house on right path narrows, pinned to field–edge. At end of wood (Channers) turn sharp left up concrete track with good views to the Chiltern Hills. Where track swings left go straight on, down two fields and turn right along hedged bridleway (Hodgedale Lane). Shortly, at end of first field on left, cross three stiles and climb grassy path beside wooden rails, then hawthorn hedge. At top turn right along drive.

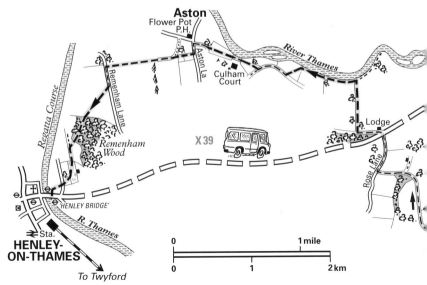

By courtesy of the Arabian owners we are able to use this Permitted Path affording wonderful views across the paddocks of the superb Juddemonte Stud, an equine paradise for the cream of English bloodstock bred here.

At drive junction turn left leading to road (Rose Lane) and turn right. Cross main road (A4130) and go left into drive at lodge. Where this prominent track swings right, follow right of way down field–edge to meadow beside River Thames. Now turn left along riverbank and follow Thames Path signs for about a mile, at one point leading across sloping lawns of Culham Court, an impressive red brick mansion built in 1771, until finally reaching a road (Aston Lane), near the popular 'Flower Pot'.

Turn *left* up the lane and immediately after Highway Cottage on right, take enclosed path uphill, then along farm track. After about ½ mile between large fields, turn left along lane and presently, at large oak, turn right through hedge and go diagonally half–left across field and into trees (Remenham Wood). Emerging, maintain direction to reach level path. Follow this to left, through small copse then along slightly raised path through middle of small golf course. After stile cross end of field, then lane, to follow railings bearing left. At main road the nearest return bus stop is a few steps away towards Henley Bridge. The bus also stops in the town centre at Market Place.

DATE WALKED | | 19

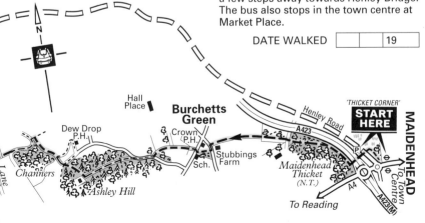

Twyford to Marlow

This unusual linear trek, over the top of Berkshire's tree–clad Bowsey Hill (452 ft.) and across the Thames into Buckinghamshire, is made possible by the Temple footbridge link (built 1989).

Distance: 10 miles
OS Maps: Explorer 3 Chiltern Hills South;
Pathfinders 1172/1173
START: Twyford Station
FINISH: Marlow Station

Leave station forecourt by path beside ticket–office. Carefully cross road, turning right over bridge and at start of hedge turn left into playing field (Stanlake Meadow). This Permitted Path follows the railway then swings right to stile by gate. Here turn left along tree–shaded lane, over railway, to bear right just before crossroads. Keep turning right and walk ahead through the pretty churchyard of St James the Great, Ruscombe.

Rejoining lane bear right over bridge (Southbury Lane). At bottom of slope, just past house on left, turn left through small field, then left again along edge of next field. Look for steps up wooded bank ahead and follow railway to road. Turn left under railway (Girder Bridge), then immediately right into bridleway between fields. About 100 yards before farmhouse fork left to road at Castle End. Bear left and cross stile by gate into field

on right. Mid–field path continues through copse then paddocks to emerge in Milley Lane, near 'Horse & Groom' at Hare Hatch.

Carefully cross main road (A4), going left and then right, into Tag Lane. Beyond a few houses, at start of wood, turn right along field edge, then over stile into woodland path. At next stile fork left along front of houses. (See map for two pubs close by.) Our path narrows and we turn left along road, then right into Bear Lane. Where road surface changes to concrete, you may need to change into a lower gear to reach sawmill. Keep to right past buildings and on into woodland. At T–junction turn left on segregated path (much improved in recent years) becoming gravel drive leading to cluster of 'away–from–it–all' properties crowning Bowsey Hill.

Just before cottage on right, turn right through gate on path beside garden which descends through woodland surrounding now hidden Cayton Park mansion. Reaching road (at Warren Row) turn right for some 60 yards, then at Hill View turn left along drive and past garage into short fenced strip. Path ahead skirts large paddock until, in front of stile, turn left and continue, beside an old hedged track (Hodgedale Lane). Finally, where path joins from left, turn right over stile, and carry on in same

The Norman parish church at Bisham

direction, now using Hodgedale Lane. It is difficult to imagine that this old way was once used by horse–drawn traffic. Those horses may have gone but the beautiful thoroughbreds in the paddocks hereabouts are the highly rated product of the Arab owned Juddemonte Stud, at Pudders Farm.

Close to path notice Hurley Chalk Pit, one of BBONT's smallest nature reserves. As path descends, white building on hilltop ahead is many–starred Danesfield Hotel. We emerge at Henley Road (A4130) opposite rather smaller but friendly 'Black Boy'. Cross main road, turning right. After

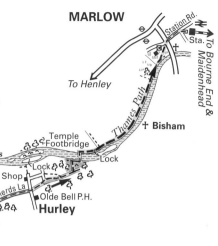

about 300 yards look for concealed stile and take the right–hand of two cross–field paths to pass left of house and join track to road. Now go straight on (Shepherd's Lane) for some distance to T–junction. This is Hurley...Rising Sun to right; shops, church and river to left.

To continue, cross ahead into fenced path. After minor road, keep straight on to end of caravan park. After stile, continue now on farm track. When level with white house, turn left into footpath and shortly right along riverside to cross the handsome Temple Footbridge (built 1989) into Buckinghamshire.

Now follow towpath for some 1½ miles, past Temple Lock and on opposite bank Bisham's 12th century All Saints Church followed by 14th century Abbey, now the Sports Council's National Recreation Centre. Approaching Marlow, look for steamer landing stage and here bear left on tarmac path through gardens of Higginson Park. *At this point allow 15 minutes to reach station.*

By park gates cross ahead into Station Road and at 'Marlow Donkey' go half–right along Station Approach to the well hidden platform.

0		1		2 miles

0	1	2	3 km

DATE WALKED | | | 19

Marlow to Henley

For centuries man has contrived to enhance the natural beauty where the Chiltern Hills meet Old Father Thames. Enjoy this procession of fine riverside estates. "It lends a precious scene to the eye." Shakespeare's words fit perfectly.

Distance: 9½ miles
OS Map: Explorer 3 Chiltern Hills South
START: Marlow Station
FINISH: Henley-on-Thames Station

Walk along Station Approach, pass right of 'Marlow Donkey' and into Station Road, leading to Marlow High Street. Here turn left along footway to left of Green. Go past church gates and cross main road where Thames Path sign leads down paved footway beside William Tierney Clark's elegant suspension bridge of 1832 (reconstructed in steel, 1964). Turn right along riverbank and shortly, where path opens out, bear away from river on broad grass strip beside railings. Cross path ahead and keep straight on along left side of sports field and in far corner pass between trees to bear left into lane.

Beyond 'Pens Place' lane dwindles to a footpath, eventually forking right to pass

Lower Ground Farm. At lodge on corner, turn left to enter Harleyford Estate along a path, enclosed at first, then straight ahead beside fence across parkland. On far side go through white kissing–gate (notice here old ice house concealed in bank) and follow wall on right at first. Signs lead through timber yard, up steps and then straight on beside golf club buildings. Path joins gravel drive, passes house, and at end of conifer hedge goes left through trees.

At path junction turn left beside flint wall and through a 75 yard long tunnel (built by a one–time Lord of the Manor beneath the lawn of 'Danesfield' – now a hotel). Our path descends to River Thames by Hurley Weir. About 25 yards beyond concrete footbridge notice near water's edge remains of the last winch (pre–1773!) used to haul boats over the former 'flash lock' just down stream. Follow narrow fenced path (past Kingfisher Lodge), then driveway, finally to reach main road (A4155).

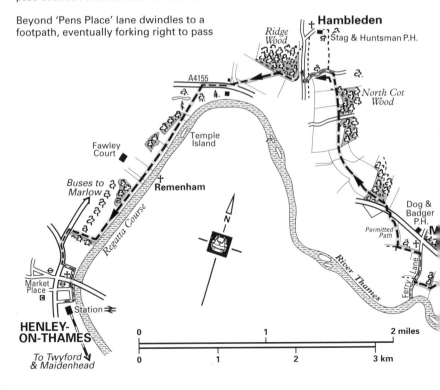

Carefully go left along road for a few paces, then turn left down drive of Abbey Lodge. When level with house turn right through swing–gate to stile and bear left through middle of field, towards left–hand end of distant wooden buildings. After stile, path crosses corner of second field and beyond footbridge continues through trees beside stream, leading to gravel area and road at Medmenham.

Now turn right along pleasant village street leading to church and nearby centuries old 'Dog & Badger'. Before church take footpath on left beside Manor House and at end of strip cross first field, then drive, and after stile ahead, immediately turn right onto 'Permissive Path', surfaced for some yards, then following headland to emerge at main road. Turn left beside broad verge, soon crossing road to climb stile lurking in corner of wood. Go up steeply rising path (Killdown Bank) and where it divides take left–hand, lower, terraced route through trees at first, then along lower slopes of open field. Cross track and continue ahead. After pair of stiles stay on same contour, neither up nor down, enjoying the superb panorama across the Thames Valley from Culham Court, looking like a doll's house on a shelf, right round to the picture book Hambleden village with the toy farmyard buildings of Mill End below. Find stile tucked in right–hand field corner, cross sunken lane and enter Hambleden Estate. After two more fields enter trees and turn sharp left down steep slope. (Here see map for link to pub/village.) At end of field join a downhill track leading to road in valley bottom. Here turn right and, after cottages, left into bridleway which tracks the contour round sheltered slopes of Ridge Wood. At second swing–gate enter field and with hedge on left at first, descend hill side to main road.

Cross over, turning right, along footway past buildings of Henley Management College. Find stile in parkland fence and follow chain of wooden footbridges linking Thames–side water meadows for some 1½ miles. At end of final meadow turn away from river. *At this point allow 30 minutes to reach station.*

At road turn left along footway. In the town turn left down New Street and follow the riverside until it bends away at Hobbs' boatyard, shortly to find railway station approach on left.

Crossing the Hambleden Valley

MARLOW

Wargrave to Henley

Visit some tucked away corners of Thames–side Wargrave before climbing gently through fields to the relative heights of Crazies Hill, of wide skies and skylarks, before free wheeling down through woodland paths to elegant Henley-on-Thames.

Distance: 6½ miles
OS Maps: Pathfinder 1172 Reading;
            Explorer 3 Chiltern Hills South
START: Wargrave Station
FINISH: Henley Station

Leaving station approach, bear right along footway (Station Road). Near far end of road, just before 'Give Way' sign, cross over and take tarmac path to right of War Memorial. (This simple, yet elegant design by Sir Edwin Lutyens, contrasts with his Cenotaph in Whitehall.) In far corner of Mill Green pass through swing–gate and along Church Street.

Cross into School Lane and after car park turn left up Backsideans. Just beyond last cottage on left turn into narrow path, soon becoming a drive. Just before end, by the bungalow 'Garth', turn right up steps to climb The Walled Garden. At top turn left into Dark Lane and bear right opposite entrance to Wargrave Manor (presently owned by the Sultan of Oman).

Follow lane (Blakes Road) until, 50 yards beyond Purfield Drive, cross over and through swing–gate. After two fields, at another gate, turn left, now with hedgerow on left. Reaching lane turn right, then immediately left, onto path through two more fields to reach road by Highfield Farm. Here turn left and just beyond entrance to Maplecroft climb bank into narrow path above road. Reaching a field, cross stile and go slightly left to metal gate in middle of far field boundary. Keep straight on through woodland to a path junction.

A few yards to right stands Rebecca's Well, a spring which used to supply the hamlet's water. This quaint well–head was built in 1870 by public subscription. However, our route goes back the other way, leading to road which we follow up through attractive cluster of properties forming Crazies Hill, complete with

Village Hall, School and Pub, but no shop!

Just after Village Hall look on left for narrow hedged footpath to the RIGHT of Summerfield House, (rebuilt here in 1900, having served as Henley's town hall for the previous century). At end of this path cross stile into field and follow the right hand fence with views of Chiltern Hills away to left. Leave first field by swing–gate in corner and continue to end of hedge on right. Cross stile and field to road at Cockpole Green.

Turn left along road until some 50 yards beyond Ashley Hill Place cross stile into field on left and head towards distant farm cottage. In next field (a private cricket ground) follow the 'boundary' ahead to reach swing–gate at roadside, opposite Pillar Lodge. Turn right along lane with good views of twin hills of Bowsey and Ashley, then left at junction with Culham Lane. Where lane bends left, beyond Upper Culham Farm, keep straight ahead on gravel track and then field edge path with hedge on right, to reach busy main road (A4130).

Here cross carefully and turn left up footway. At top of slope turn right along track towards fields. At end of garden on left, turn left and follow headland behind properties on left to emerge finally at the corner of Aston Lane.

Turn right down lane and just past last house on right, take footpath on left, with fields flowing away like sea shore rollers. When path becomes stony track, look on right for entrance to 'Common Barn' and enter narrow path to left of gate post. This leads through light woodland, giving way to open views across river valley. Go through weighted wicket gate and turn slightly left past one or two mid–field trees. Keep on same line in next field and at lane turn left, then immediately right over stile into Remenham Woods.

Look out for prominent crossing track and 30 yards beyond, be sure to fork left down way marked path which soon narrows between railings, finally descending to roadside (White Hill). Follow footway down to Henley Bridge. (The massive causeway carrying the road – notice how steep the sides are –

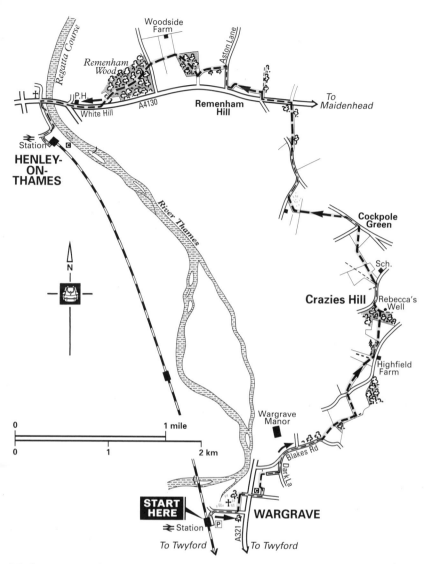

Woodside Farm

Remenham Wood

Regatta Course

P.H.

White Hill

A4130

Remenham Hill

Aston Lane

To Maidenhead

Station

HENLEY-ON-THAMES

River Thames

N

Cockpole Green

Sch.

Crazies Hill

Rebecca's Well

Highfield Farm

Wargrave Manor

Blakes Rd

Dark La.

0   1 mile

0   1   2 km

START HERE

Station

To Twyford

P

A321

WARGRAVE

To Twyford

Join the regatta crowds on Henley Bridge

was built around 1770 by Humphrey Gainsborough, brother of the artist Thomas, to reduce the steepness of the hill.) Turn left at traffic lights by the Angel on the Bridge. Follow riverside until it bends away by Hobbs boatyard and shortly find railway station approach on left.

DATE WALKED

| | | 19 |

Maidenhead to Twyford

Take this easy stroll through a tapestry of English history, woven of matchless Manors, their churches, farms and parkland.

Distance: 9½ miles
OS Map: Pathfinder 1173 Windsor
START: Maidenhead Station
FINISH: Twyford Station

Leave station subway by Platform 1 and turn right (Shoppenhangers Road). At first traffic island cross over and follow the footway up past golf club entrance, then along wide verge, finally bearing left into Manor Road. At junction bear left again, cross over and just beyond No. 12 turn right into broad path leading to another road. Here turn left and soon catch glimpses of the old Shoppenhangers Manor, now a hotel.

Where the footway ends turn right down narrow lane (Spring Hill). Bearing right brings us to a footbridge over the A423(M). On far side immediately turn left into narrow fenced path leading to Ockwells Park. Follow left–hand hedge to far corner and then go straight on to reach a bridge (built by East Berks Ramblers in 1975 and, like the Group, still going strong!). Continue with fence on right, to cross stile in field corner. For the next few minutes switch off your hearing aid until normal conversation can be resumed!

At end of wood (Little Thrift) turn right along track and when this bends right, go straight on, now on field edge. At end of trees turn right over footbridge. Path crosses field ahead and rejoins headland leading to far corner, going straight into Great Thrift Wood to reach T–junction. Ahead lies the 474 ft summit of Ashley Hill.

Turn left alongside ditch, then hedge, leading to Heywood Farm. Use track past farm buildings, then, ignoring a path turning left, go straight on between fields. At concrete track, turn left for 30 yards, then right, to go straight ahead across field. Notice parkland (Waltham Place) with its beautiful old trees, sweeping down to village church and cottages of White Waltham.

Leaving field at stile, immediately turn left between trees, then left up footway and through St Mary's churchyard, admiring the immense Sequoia. Rejoining footway for about 100 yards, with especial care cross over and up some brick steps to enter Love Path, terraced at first, then down a meadow to road opposite the rebuilt Grove House. You may like to celebrate reaching nearly halfway by taking a breather in adjoining Waltham Grove Field, a useful vantage point for viewing the occasional flying display over nearby airfield!

Now continue through the village and take path straight across cricket green

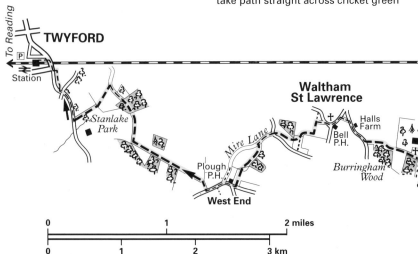

to gap in fence. This leads across the wide acres of historic Shottesbrooke Park, passing to left of the tiny, immaculate, medieval church of St John, little changed since completed in 1337. Beyond church our path continues over stiles,through two fields and a small wood to reach a road (Halls Lane).

Here turn right and at Halls Farm turn left, soon narrowing between gardens to rejoin Halls Lane, turning left to centre of Waltham St Lawrence. Unless adjourning to the church or the 'Bell' (of equal interest) pass between the Pound and Neville Hall and within a few paces

'The Bell' at Waltham St. Lawrence

bear left into Neville Close. At far end turn left across open field and then right along headland. After stile bear right past oak and head for far left–hand corner of long field where a hidden stile plugs the hedge.

Look and listen carefully before crossing road into track (Mire Lane). Soon after concrete bridge enter first field on left and follow left side. After stile, path bisects next field to cross footbridge. Walk over the brow of meadow and in far corner turn right past the 'Plough', at West End. Keep along this lane as far as gates of 'Blackthorn'. Here turn right into bridleway, concrete at first, then between poplars. Stay along edge of two very large fields (which once formed part of Ruscombe Lake until drained in the 1820's). Finally, the way passes through woodland strip to emerge at roadway (Southbury Lane), by Ferryman's Cottage.

At next property, 'Thatched Cottage', turn left and take a straight, level, midfield line to reach parkland surrounding Stanlake House (built 1580's). Follow fence line and at road turn right up footway. At roundabout cross Stanlake Lane and bear left before entering playing field, by pavilion. Keep to left–hand side to far corner and rejoin road. Just beyond railway bridge cross road into station path.

DATE WALKED [   ] [19]

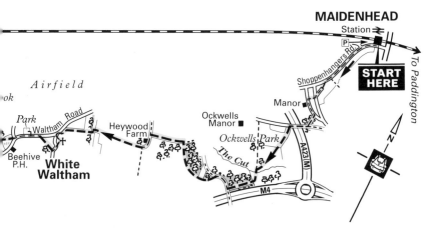

Reading to Shiplake

Enjoy a draught of Reading's dramatic history; share the views from today's high tech pavilions; but save your breath for a modest scramble up a Chiltern hill!

Distance: 8½ miles
OS Map: Pathfinder 1172 Reading
START: Reading Station
FINISH: Shiplake Station

From main concourse (Brunel Arcade) follow signs 'Heathrow passengers'. At coach bay use pedestrian crossing over main road, turning left and first right into Blagrave Street. Cross to front of splendid red brick Town Hall & Museum.

Mid-field path with distant views of Bowsey Hill

Follow front of Town Hall (with Queen Victoria surveying the Square), and take path to left of St Lawrence's Church, once part of the great Reading Abbey. At end of churchyard cross busy road and go through gate ahead. Cross middle of Forbury Gardens to far right corner and pass under low flint bridge.

Entering Abbey ruins our route lies ahead on tarmac path to right, but a few minutes exploring is well worthwhile. Reaching River Kennet ahead, turn left along Chestnut Walk. Follow riverside path under road bridge, then turn sharp left, back over bridge and rejoin waterside by the imposing Prudential buildings. Use pretty footbridge here to visit small island hosting life size bronze by Kenneth Atherton, based on a local fisherman. When without his fishing rod, as at present, sadly the 'Incomplete Angler'!

A short passage leads from river to road. Here turn right, then left, passing facade of Huntley & Palmer's former head office. Descend steps on left and now with canal on left follow Kennet Side for about half a mile, passing Blake's Lock, to reach Kennet Mouth, confluence with River Thames. Note here, attached to Brunel's railway bridge, quaint wooden structure known as Horseshoe Bridge which enabled barge–horses to continue along towpath.

Turn downstream and enjoy the varied river scenery for next two miles to Sonning. Within the first mile pass an old house, once the Dreadnought pub. Thames Valley Park and a nature reserve have replaced Earley Power Station and various factories; a great improvement.

After Sonning Lock, the 'Promenade' leads to hump backed 18th century bridge. Cross river and when opposite 'French Horn' take narrow tarmac Furleigh Path behind car park, then turn left and right on quiet lane through Sonning Eye (meaning 'island'). At next junction keep straight on to end of cul–de–sac and cross busy road (B478) into Poolspring

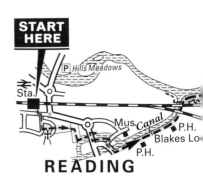

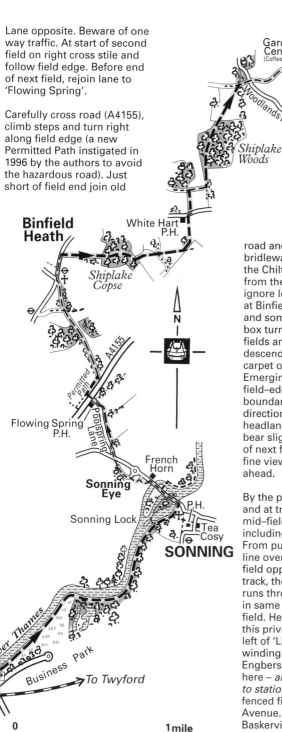

Lane opposite. Beware of one way traffic. At start of second field on right cross stile and follow field edge. Before end of next field, rejoin lane to 'Flowing Spring'.

Carefully cross road (A4155), climb steps and turn right along field edge (a new Permitted Path instigated in 1996 by the authors to avoid the hazardous road). Just short of field end join old

road and turn sharp left on bridleway up south eastern face of the Chiltern Hills as they billow up from the valley. Keep climbing, ignore left fork, finally to reach road at Binfield Heath. Here turn right and some 90 paces beyond post box turn right down side of two fields and into Shiplake Copse, on descending woodland path – a carpet of bluebells in May. Emerging from trees bear left along field–edge. Shortly, where field boundary swings left, maintain direction across field, to regain headland. Cross sunken track and bear slightly right through middle of next field to electricity–pole, with fine views, including Bowsey Hill, ahead.

By the post turn left between fields and at tree clump bear left mid–field towards buildings, including the popular 'White Hart'. From pub car park follow hedge line over road and along left side of field opposite. Turn right on gravel track, then left at junction. This path runs through wood and continues in same direction to far corner of field. Here turn right and at end of this private road go straight on, to left of 'Little Beeches', down winding bridleway to main road by Engbers garden centre. Coffee shop here – *allow fifteen minutes to station.* Cross road and take fenced field path to Northfield Avenue. At junction opposite Baskerville Arms turn left to nearby Shiplake Station.

DATE WALKED 19

Reading to Pangbourne

While Reading turns its back on the Thames, Caversham welcomes walkers with the green grandstand of Christchurch Meadows as we saunter towards the tranquil Tudor estates of Mapledurham and Hardwick.

Distance: 8 miles
OS Map: PATHFINDER 1172 Reading
START: Reading Station or Hills Meadow car park (Grid ref: 719741 – free parking pm Sat & all day on Sunday).
FINISH: Pangbourne Station

FROM READING STATION: On station footbridge follow 'Caversham & River Thames' sign. Take lift to ground and go diagonally right across car park to pedestrian road crossing. Follow railings ahead onto footway over Reading Bridge and on far side descend steps to riverbank.

FROM CAR PARK: Join riverside path leading under Reading Bridge.

Now follow the broad path up stream through Christchurch Meadows. (The mid stream island along here was the scene of a duel between Robert de Montfort and Henry of Essex in 1157.) Finally, path leaves river to right of War Memorial. At end of service road turn right down to traffic lights. Cross over

and up Church Road to enter wrought iron gates (one–time gardens of Caversham Court). From entrance bear right on stone path and up steps to pass beside St Peter's Church.

Turn left down road (The Warren) and follow for just over a mile past an interesting selection of riverside properties built since prosperous Victorians first 'colonised' the area. At far end of tarmac road continue on gravel track for another 200 yards, then turn very sharp right up gulley to emerge in Blagrave Lane at top of hill.

Just past old white cottage bear left along bridleway (Jacksons Lane). Ignoring a left branch, continue on tree–lined bridleway which eventually widens, leading to another white cottage, thatched this time. Turn left on concrete track and after 60 yards go right over stile *(N.B. Plans afoot for golf courses here!)*. This mid–field path crosses valley ahead, and with recently planted trees on left, exit this second field by stile. Here turn right and follow the path, keeping the copse (Noke End Shaw), on your left. This grassy path takes us through Rose Farm, becoming a concrete drive.

Where drive divides, keep straight on across field ahead and then through

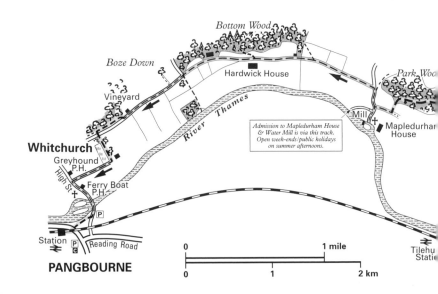

The watermill at Mapledurham

mature trees (Park Wood). On far side ignore track to right but turn left down grassy path. Since the devastating storm of October, 1987 the hillside has been completely replanted with oak, ash and beech. Follow winding path down past monument, leading to stile. Cross field ahead and turn right along concrete farm track to reach road. To left lies the quintessentially English village of Mapledurham with its Elizabethan mansion, cottages, church and watermill.

To continue our walk turn away up lane from village and shortly left at White House (once the 'King's Arms' until closed by a Victorian Lord of the Manor). This bridleway runs through the Hardwick Estate, passing the mansion house, seen over a hedge. Like Mapledurham, the house is also Tudor –

keeping up with the neighbours perhaps. In fact, Queen Elizabeth slept in both of them, so honours were even!

On our right, by the house, are a row of brick built air raid shelters provided in WW2 when it served as a hospital. Unusually, there are two 'real tennis' courts in the grounds. One, now dilapidated, is visible on left of drive. Further along we pass a fine stable yard built about 1900 by Sir Charles Rose, one–time MP for Newmarket. His stud farm here bred the mare Cyllene, the 1899 winner of the Ascot Gold Cup, amongst whose progeny is the top stallion Northern Dancer. Today, this is a livery stable.

Reaching gates at end of drive notice a path to left. This leads within a few minutes to a secluded spot on the riverbank, ideal for a picnic. Continuing along the road (Hardwick Road) the next point of interest is the buildings formerly called Bozedown Farm, now a vineyard (free tastings at weekends). From here use the raised footpath, Jubilee Walk (Queen's Silver 1977), until rejoining road, then cross over and pass to side of wooden gate and down tree lined track. At end of cricket ground on right, turn right along road (Eastfield Lane), to reach Whitchurch village by the Greyhound and turn left.

At this point allow ten minutes to reach station. If there is time to spare you may take a small detour following Thames Path signs shortly on right. The direct route is along village street, over toll bridge and, just beyond Pangbourne's imposing new surgery, turn right on narrow tarmac path. Cross gravel drive, pass newly–built Waterside House (note small public riverside garden), then along drive to main road and Station.

DATE WALKED | | 19

Pangbourne to Goring

A necklace of Chiltern woods and copses provide shade in summer and shelter in winter as our route goes up, down and roundabout; a walk for all seasons.

Distance: 5½ miles
OS Maps: Pathfinder 1172 Reading;
Explorer 3 Chiltern Hills
START: Pangbourne Station
FINISH: Goring Station

From Pangbourne Station walk down to main road and from north side of railway bridges with utmost care cross Shooters Hill to enter railed path ahead, alongside drive. Path goes between new Waterside House and river to emerge at road.

Turn left along footway leading over Whitchurch's Victorian iron toll–bridge (pedestrians free). One of only two such bridges left on the Thames, it replaces a wooden one built in 1799. Immediately beyond bridge turn left and in front of mill turn right along walled path. Pass church and follow drive to rejoin road. Continue up village street past 'Greyhound'. At top of village bear left up narrower road, then shortly make use of full length of raised verge on right before crossing road to War Memorial opposite.

Continue uphill for some yards and, as road swings away to right, go straight up slope through swing–gate and along left field–edge (beside Stoneycroft Plantation). At end of field, go through swing–gate and along broad grass track, passing to right of Beech Farm buildings (at this point an unauthorised diversion of the definitive line). Cross concrete drive and through paddock to swing–gate ahead into wood. Where path divides bear right, along twisting line caused by neglect of this otherwise attractive woodland. Leaving wood, follow line of chestnut trees beside drive to road from Boundary Farm.

Turn right for a few yards, then left, through wide gap in hedge. Go slightly left on midfield line across first field, then aim just to left of distant cottage. Here turn right along lane and shortly fork left by Laurel Cottage. Follow the lane through pretty hamlet of Coldharbour until, with property ahead, our way turns sharp right, downhill into woodland.

On reaching a track, turn left for a few yards, then right up bank and follow enclosed path to right of field ahead. In next field, bear slightly left to exit by gap in hedge, crossing lane (B4526) into bridleway opposite. Where bridleway emerges from woodland, look left for view down to historic Elvendon Priory. Meeting road, turn left for a hundred yards, then right, along another bridleway, soon beside long field. Where this pleasant chalk track turns away,

The chalk track to Wroxhills Plantation

don't be led astray! Keep straight on, now on grassy path beside fence, to end of field, before plunging into trees (Wroxhills Plantation). Eventually, still in woodland, on reaching a crossing path, turn sharp left down steadily increasing slope. Sweeping vistas open up towards Goring Gap and Lardon Chase (see Ramble 16).

Reaching road, turn right for 20 paces, then left, into long woodland strip. Look for stile ahead and maintain same direction through bottom of field and over two further stiles straight ahead. Emerging at minor road, cross over bearing left on tarmac path leading into Lockstile Way.

Where Valley Close joins from left, cross ahead into narrow path on right of No. 2. Shortly bear right to reach main road (B4009). Here turn left for Goring Station or over bridge ahead to village and river.

DATE WALKED

		19

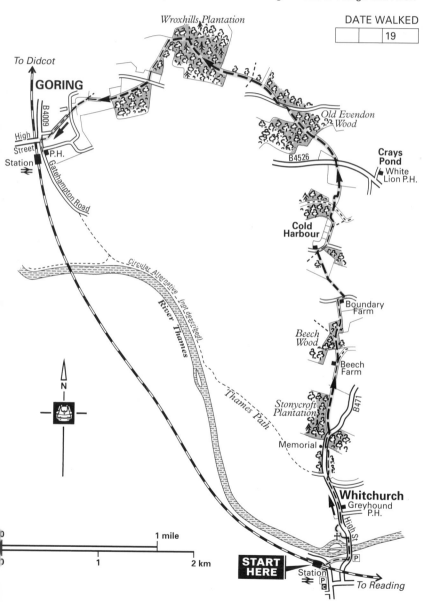

Goring/Streatley Circular

A challenging roller coaster of a walk encircling the National Trust's 'Holies' estate, with stunning vistas from Lardon Chase and Lough Down.

Distance: 6 miles
OS Maps: Explorer 3 Chiltern Hills south
        & parts of Pathfinder 1155,
        1171 & 1172
START/FINISH: Goring Station

From station footbridge turn left along Platform 1 with barrier on right. At road go straight ahead (Station Road) beside old barn. At junction with Manor Road, by 'John Barleycorn', cross straight ahead into narrow Ferry Lane leading to the Thames. A Roman causeway here was usable until Goring Lock was built in 1787, the water deepened and a ferry started.

Turn up–stream along Thames Path. Facing recently refurbished Streatley Bridge (original wooden bridge of 1837 was replaced in 1926 by this concrete one) turn right and just beyond Gallery (part of mill) mount steps, cross road and turn left over river. This is the site of a most important prehistoric ford linking the Icknield Way to the Ridgeway. Just after the 'Swan' (note the old Magdalen College barge moored nearby) cross back over road to enter Vicarage Lane. Just before Old Vicarage, take footpath on right which twists and turns up to main road (A329). Turn left along footway until shortly after end of roadside fencing, carefully cross to steps up bank and continue in same direction on new woodland path, instigated in 1997 by the authors, through Holies Walk Wood.

This wood forms part of the Holies, some 48 hectares of species rich pasture, heathland and woodland, presented to the NT in 1988 following a public appeal. It adjoins the NT Lardon Chase and Lough Down. Local names such as Holies Walk and Papist Bushes may well be connected with the Catholic family of Buriton who held Streatley Manor after the dissolution of the monasteries. A Thomas Buriton was buried in the church in 1603.

At end of woodland head across bottom of meadow. Exit through swing–gate and join bridleway climbing steeply up wooded gulley. At the top, path cuts through chalk bank of Grimm's Ditch.

This is an impressive earthwork running to Tring in Hertfordshire, the origin of which the experts can only disagree about! Our way descends tarmac drive beside bank of Ditch, crosses a road, and continues down, then up, valley ahead. Where road bends left, bear right onto level path (Stitchen's Green) becoming a very stony track descending to pass house and stable buildings of Wood Farm.

Here go left along road and just past Red Cottage turn right into field. Within a few yards pass through gap into adjoining field and continue uphill, with distant views towards Reading. At top corner go straight on up, now with woodland on right. At field corner cross stile and turn left, along fringe of Common Wood. At next stile path dips to right, then continues on level ground; this is now Parsonage Wood. Bear right along drive to reach road (top of Streatley Hill). Cross over and in far left–hand corner of car park find path at gate, leading onto Lardon Chase. Strolling over this well trodden turf affords memorable views over the Goring Gap as old Father Thames squeezes between the Berkshire Downs and the chalk hills of the Chilterns.

At corner of hedge turn left through swing–gate onto Lough Down (NT) with northerly views towards Wittenham Clumps on horizon (Iron Age hill fort, see Ramble 20). Keep to middle of Down, aiming for white house at dip in field-edge below, where swing–gate leads to road and we turn right, joining the long distance Ridgeway Path. At junction (Wantage Road) turn left crossing over, then shortly right, down Townsend Road. Again, turn left crossing over and in a few yards pass beside metal gate into gravel drive leading to riverside meadow, within sight of Cleeve Lock. Now turn right, along Thames Path.

Entering small meadow, path bears away from river, over footbridge and onto causeway. This leads to minor road which passes St. Mary's Church and Village Hall (converted from malthouse in 1898), to reach High Street. Retrace your steps over river. *At this point allow 15 minutes to reach station*. Goring High St. ahead leads to railway bridge. Turn right to station.

DATE WALKED | | 19

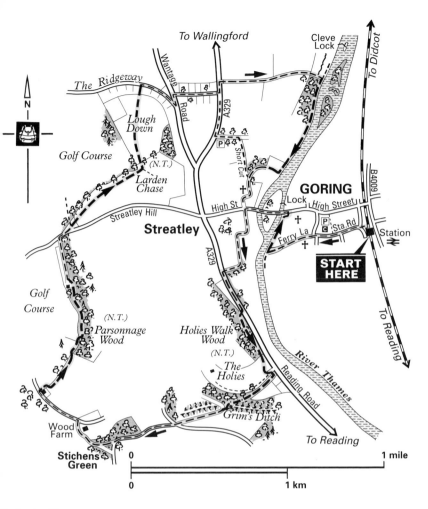

To Wallingford

Cleve Lock

To Didcot

The Ridgeway

Wantage Road

A329

Lough Down

Golf Course

(N.T.)

Larden Chase

P

Short Cut

GORING

Streatley Hill

High St

Lock

High Street

Sta. Rd

B4009

Station

Streatley

A329

Ferry La

P

START HERE

To Reading

Golf Course

(N.T.)

Parsonnage Wood

Holies Walk Wood

(N.T.)

The Holies

River Thames

Reading Road

Wood Farm

Grim's Ditch

To Reading

Stichens Green

N

0 ——————————————— 1 mile

0 ——————————————— 1 km

On Lardon Chase

Cholsey to Goring ~ *via Chilterns*

Forget our crazy world on this pilgrimage over the hills to remote Hailey and historic Ipsden. Your steps will leave no trace but the scenery may be imprinted on your mind for many a long day!

Distance: 11¾ miles
OS Maps: Pathfinder 1155 Wantage/
          Didcot; Explorer 3 Chiltern
          Hills South
START: Cholsey Station
FINISH: Goring Station

Leaving station building, immediately turn left down narrow fenced path. Continue ahead along estate road (West End) until, opposite Sandy Way, turn left into footpath between houses. After first rail tunnel turn sharp right along field path beside private line (trains operated by Cholsey and Wallingford Railway Preservation Society on Sundays, from Mar – Sept, details tel: 01491 835 067). At end of first field cross double stile and head towards Cholsey's 12th century Church of St Mary, built by the monks of Reading Abbey.

Cross graveyard (Agatha Christie is buried here in NW corner) towards Norman south door. Go to right of church and out to road. Take cross–field path beside The Hazels, to stile in far corner, again beside rail–line. Continue through several fields (about a mile) until path joins track from farm and crosses line to bypass. Cross this road and turn right along its wide grass verge. Use roadside footway to pass left of two roundabouts and continue ahead over river bridge. On far side follow path dipping down to left. Turn right to pass under road and (remounting your horse!) keep straight on, joining the Ridgeway Path through Carmel College. For a rewarding 5 minute detour here, take public path through the lovely grounds to visit picturesque riverside ruin of St John's Church.

Our route continues along the Ridgeway Path until just past end of college buildings, at start of second field, we turn left into Mongewell Park. *At this point the Ridgeway Path offers a shorter alternative to the end of our walk (see map).* At top of park bear right to cross road and enter swing–gate to climb bridleway. After another right and left

Cholsey to Wallingford branch line

over road (Port Way, a Roman road) bridleway continues up chalk slope to isolated Sheepcot Farm.

Turn left along track, then right between barns. Just past silo keep left into field ahead, with hedge on right. Go straight on, through bridle–gate in far hedgerow, across middle of next field, then over lane into gravel track. Cross next lane and go ahead towards Woodhouse Farm until, just before the typical old Chiltern farmhouse, turn right up bank into trees (Wicks Wood). Path continues across open meadow, then joins track past Poors Farm, to emerge by Stone Farm in the hamlet of Hailey. A perfect country pub stands a few yards to left, folded in the green arms of this remote place. It marks the halfway point of our odyssey.

To continue, go down the lane from Hailey. Just past post–box take path bearing left across corner of <u>two</u> fields and through middle of a third, with Ipsden's tiny church away on right. At far corner of this field bear left down bridleway, crossing road (notice beautiful Georgian rectory). At group of sarsen stones ahead bear right beside cricket green, then right down lane to Ipsden Farm with longest traditional barn (365 ft) in England! Follow lane beside barn and at copse cross ditch onto Swans Way, also route of prehistoric Icknield Way, by remains of

Layend Pond (notice monument to a Victorian son of the Manor).

Go midfield ahead and cross main road, turning right along verge. Some 50 yards before 'Ipsden' sign turn left onto newly opened mile long path through open fields traversing hill ahead. This path crosses bridleway in new plantation on high ground (Watch Folly) then descends to join lane towards South Stoke village.

At road junction, go ahead along Ferry Road and turn left along wall of Manor Farm, then pass St Andrew's Church and 'Pike & Perch'. Where road swings left at end of village go straight on, rejoining our friend the Ridgeway Path which leads us the last 1½ miles, past the 'Leatherne Bottel' and Cleeve Mill. Finally, at main road in Goring, *allowing 15 minutes to reach station*, turn left up High Street.

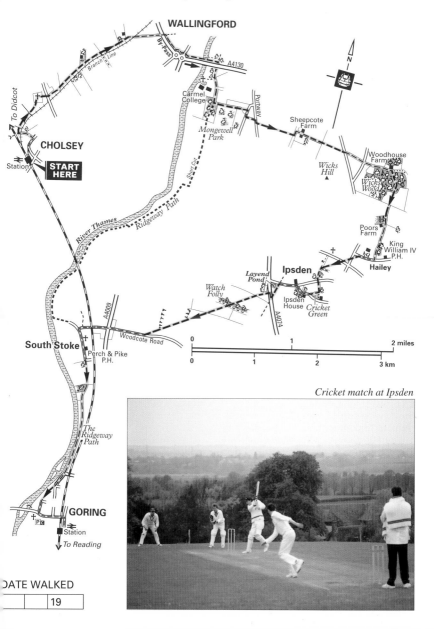

Cricket match at Ipsden

Cholsey to Goring
~ *via Berkshire Downs*

Old, older, oldest road? No one can be sure about the Ridgeway. But for thousands of years man has used this downland highway, built forts along it, worshipped beside it, been buried near it. You can share its aura. So, up, up and away!

Distance: 11¾ miles
OS Map: Pathfinder 1155
          Wantage/Didcot (mainly)
START: Cholsey Station
FINISH: Goring Station

Leaving station building, immediately turn left down narrow fenced path. Continue ahead along estate road (West End) until, opposite Sandy Lane, turn left into footpath between houses. Path goes through two rail tunnels. After the second of these, facing white rails, fork left through middle of field to footbridge. From here path runs straight ahead through three flat arable fields, followed by two meadows, to reach farm drive. Turn right and at end of field on left, go left into wide grass track. Do notice the splendid trotting horse weather vane on the granary here of Lollingdon Farm.

Track climbs shoulder of Lollingdon Hill (314 ft) with fine views. *Start to descend the other side of hill but at end of field on right, turn right, along grass headland. Continue in next field until track bends left (to Carrimers Farm). Here go straight on across field corner and carefully maintain direction along road ahead (A417). Beyond white house on brow of hill turn left onto track. Soon, where this bears off left, we bear right, to find almost hidden entrance to hedged bridleway, with fields either side. Emerging into field continue ahead on track beside field boundary above valley (Chalk Hill Bottom).

At end of field, exit through gateway and go ahead on steadily climbing chalk byway. At crossing track (The Fair Mile to left) go straight on, soon rising, with historic Lowbury Hill (610 ft), site of Roman Temple and tumulus, nearby on right. Where trees thin (highest point on track) join footpath straight ahead (now in Berkshire) – a perfect downland way of thickly cushioned grass and a great view to match!

Our path now joins the ancient Ridgeway. Ignore first turning left (to Warren Farm) and byway to right, then at fork bear left. (If needs be, the Ridgeway ahead offers a short cut to Goring.) The drive we have joined enters Well Barn Estate. In front of property, go left over stile and take left of two paths, clearly waymarked. (The ridge through Town Copse here marks boundary between Berkshire and Oxfordshire.) Leaving wood ignore track bearing right and go straight on down headland with fence on left.

Continue down steep drive facing Fullers Firs on hillside ahead. At bottom of slope, path bears right, across field to gap in hedge near lowest point. From here path, hopefully easily discernible, traces the floor of this stunning tree–fringed valley (Unhill Bottom) eventually joining drive to Starveall Farm, there kinking left, leading to road. Here path line goes straight on over road and along broad grass track beside aptly–named Badger Bank. (In 1960, just north of here, a Bronze Age Torque was found while ploughing. Made of gold and weighing 1lb, it is held by Reading Museum.) Pass between wooden rails into woodland strip and then straight across playing field to hedged parking area. Cross road turning right, in front of impressive old village house (Moulsford Grange) and take first on left, Ferry Lane, to river by 'Beetle & Wedge'. (While staying here around 1910, H. G. Wells wrote 'The History of Mr Polly'; the hotel inspired his description of the Potwell Inn.)

At water's edge turn downstream and follow Thames Path into open meadows with view of South Stoke across the river. The 'Olde Leatherne Bottel' appears on far bank, soon followed by Cleeve Lock. *From here allow 30 minutes to reach Goring Station.* Stay on the riverside along fenced section until entering small meadow, path bears away from river and crosses footbridge to causeway. This leads to minor road which passes Saint Mary's Church and Village Hall to reach High Street, Streatley. Turn left and cross river bridges. Follow Goring's High Street leading to railway bridge and the station

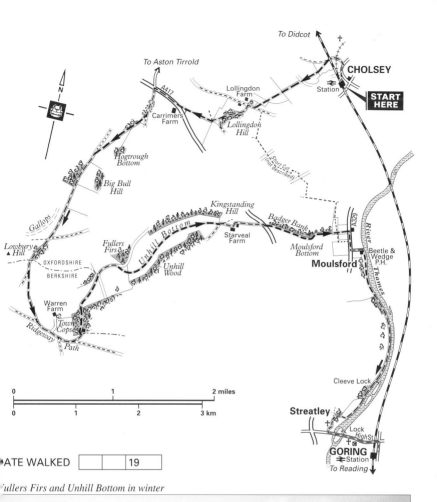

Fullers Firs and Unhill Bottom in winter

Didcot to Cholsey

Dreary Didcot – but gateway to paradise! Or, more exactly, to a chain of Oxfordshire's delectable Vale of the White Horse villages. From tiny Upton to bountiful Blewbury, all are ready to reveal their secrets to the inquiring foot traveller.

Distance: 8½ miles
OS Maps: Pathfinder 1136 Abingdon & 1155 Wantage/Didcot
START: Didcot Station
FINISH: Cholsey Station

From station forecourt turn right and shortly cross road to enter footpath

beside Cronshaw Close. At open space turn left between graveyards leading to Didcot's old hilltop church. Here cross road ahead into tarmac path beside timbered Rectory Cottage and cross two minor roads. At main road turn right to roundabout. Cross ahead into Wantage Road. At parade of shops, cross road to enter narrow footpath, (an old route marked by mature trees). At end of tarmac surface, just ½ hour easy walking from station, this first stile marks start of our countryside!

At end of first field, path twists round hedge in front and continues on between fields with distant view towards Churn Hill. At junction of paths bear left between metal gates on concrete track until, just before bend, cross stile to pass left of barn. At corner of barn path goes straight across concrete apron, over field, through tiny orchard and down steps beside pretty white cottage emerging in York Road, West Hagbourne.

Follow road signed to Upton and where this swings right, go ahead past pond, turn left, then first right, onto broad grass path between paddocks. From stile, midfield path bears right towards long embankment of dismantled railway (old GWR line from Didcot to Newbury & Southampton, opened 1882). The definitive (official) path goes under the old line but our route climbs the embankment, then turns right along the top, to enable us to admire the view. At end of field below on left, go down steep path and across playing field, past hall, turning left down road into tiny village of Upton.

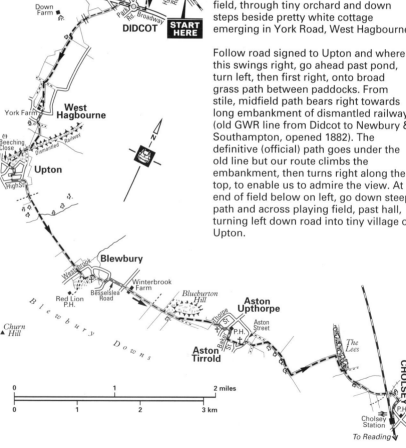

turn right into Pound Lane and right again into Stream Road where, within 5 yards, turn left along narrow path. At road turn left. Follow it past Manor House, becoming gravel track then finally grass, beside orchard. Stay on this well preserved old path ahead for a mile to reach Blewbury, beloved by writers, artists and racing men!

At roadside (Westbrook St.) go left, then directly right, soon beside that special feature of this village, one of the thatched cob walls. Crossing Mill Brook brings us to secluded village green. Blewbury's oldest pub, the 'Red Lion', is two minutes away, across green to right. To continue our route, however, follow left edge of green to join paved path. This leads past some pretty gardens, the Almshouse and the church. The Vicar here from 1782 to 1824 became known as Blewbury Jones the Miser. He always visited parishioners at meal times in the hope of a free meal! When he died he left £18,000 – a large sum in those days.)

After the church, by Watts Spring, turn right. At road (South Street) turn left, then first right, Try *not* to notice the striking property on left called 'Y–Worry'! At end of Besselslea Road cross over and continue on concrete road, passing Winterbrook Farm. Our way lies beside the Iron–age fort on Blewburton Hill ahead. When almost beyond hill, cross stile on left and follow feint downland way, keeping left to swing–gate marking entrance to twin villages of Aston Upthorpe and Aston Tirrold.

Descend stony track and turn right on road (Thorpe St.) past church. Turn left down Spring Lane, then to right of 'The Chequers' in Baker St. At end of field on left, turn left into hedged path leading into St Michael's churchyard, Aston Tirrold. Turn left down lane beyond church, then right into footpath opposite black boarded barn. At stile ahead go half left across field and through gap in boundary, bearing right on concrete track. Path goes on beside stream until at end of field on left, turn left and follow ditch round two long sides of big field. Just before far corner, turn left over railed footbridge, then right along field edge. About half way along field cross plank bridge and continue, now with deep ditch to right. From white metal rails path crosses under two rail tunnels to arrive at road (West End). Here turn right and where road bends left, join enclosed path beside embankment leading to station.

DATE WALKED [   ] [19]

Wallingford to Dorchester
~ *via Brightwell*

Before the bulldozer man did things the hard way. Cross the Saxon defences of a Royal Borough, then over the Downs to an Iron Age fort and on to the man made Dyke Hills. Truly a walk back in history.

Distance: 8 miles
OS Maps: Explorer 3 Chiltern Hills South;
         Pathfinders 1136 Abingdon &
         1155 Wantage/Didcot
START: Market Place, Wallingford
FINISH: Bus stop near Dorchester Abbey

Facing the pillared open fronted Town Hall (built 1670), walk to right and when level with porch of St Mary's Church, cross the one–way road into Church Lane, soon becoming Kinecroft. Path continues straight ahead over open green (a bank and ditch here are remains of Saxon defences) and on into Cross Villas. At metal barrier turn right into narrow tarmac path to cross an estate road and continues beside industrial buildings. At next estate road (Fir Tree Avenue) cross over, turning right. Pass six houses, then turn left. At entrance to allotments go through swing–gate and continue ahead, eventually entering field. Keep alongside hedge to reach and cross by–pass.

From footbridge follow cross–field path ahead, passing pole on far side. Turn right over stile into next field and follow field edge with ditch on right and occasional trees. (At a stile look right for glimpse of spire of tiny St James' Church, Sotwell.) Stay on field edge to swing gate in corner, then across sports field to road, turning right into the delightful village of Brightwell-cum-Sotwell.

On the corner ahead the 'Red Lion' beckons but the immediate attraction of this delectable pair of villages, and the

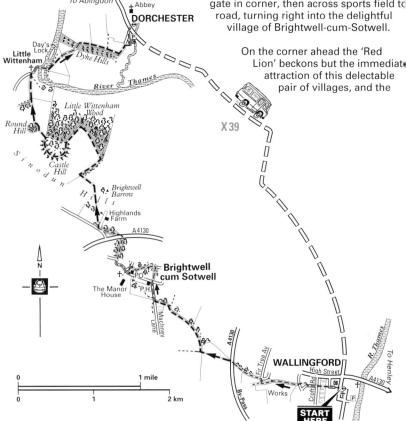

envy of many others, is the absence of through traffic and consequent tranquillity. It is tempting to spend an hour or so just wandering round the back lanes, admiring the cottages and houses of all styles and periods, listening to the silence!

For a flavour of its delights, from Mackney Lane cross into bridleway fronting Moat Cottage. Small bridge leads to tiny pond (called Sat Well). Here turn left along path, to pass recreation ground, and emerge at roadside. Turn left to find The Square, with War Memorial, post office stores and entrance to St Agatha's Church.

Turn right along West End past village hall and follow footway round first road bend. At second bend, cross straight ahead into tree sheltered track. At the top, possibly with difficulty, cross the busy by–pass, turning left between fence, now along the 'old' road. At Highlands Farm entrance, find stile at field corner. Take the diagonal fieldpath up the Sinodun Hills (crossing two stiles) with views behind improving with every stride, from the Chiltern Hills, across the Goring Gap, to the Berkshire Downs.

At cattle trough, with O.S. pillar marking Brightwell Barrow away on right, turn left and walk down towards Castle Hill.

Alas, the direct route enjoyed by past generations is no more and we must trudge round three sides of the next field to access the Iron-age fort on Castle Hill. To share the tremendous views enjoyed by its builders 4,000 years ago and every generation since, walk clockwise round the outer bank. At a crossing path, go ahead onto the downland and up to the smaller fenced beech–clump on Round Hill. Follow fence to right and at Viewpoint head downhill to distant church of Little Wittenham.

Here turn right down track towards Day's Lock. Cross river footbridge and turn half–left over meadow to enter narrow path between fields, then beside an ancient earth work called Dyke Hills (town defences). At end of these low hills the way bends left and opposite The Thatched Cottage a short path leads down to pretty cluster of houses. Keep left of green and continue ahead (along Bridge End) to reach, hopefully with enough time and energy left to explore a little of this wonderful Roman town of Dorchester, once the capital of the Kingdom of Wessex.

DATE WALKED | | 19

Wallingford to Dorchester
~ via Benson

This is a difficult walk! You may be beguiled by Benson, seduced by Berrick Salome, waylaid by Warborough. Great concentration is needed to reach the end in Dorchester, the 'most historic town in Oxfordshire'.

Distance: 8 miles
OS Maps: Explorer 3 Chiltern Hills South; Pathfinder 1136 Abingdon
START: Market Place, Wallingford
FINISH: Bus stop near Dorchester Abbey

With your back to Town Hall, walk across Market Place (once a bull ring!) past a Victorian drinking fountain, to far corner and into paved St Marys St. Cross High St. turning left, then right, into Castle St. (The old building here with jettied first–floor, was part of the 'Lamb', an ancient hostelry. In 1688 William of Orange was entertained here en–route to London to receive the Crown.)

Shortly ahead turn right at sign to Castle Gardens, normally open every day from 10 am. If closed, use footpath (Castle Lane) further along Castle St. Inside gardens follow path across what was the moat and up steps, to turn right along grassy ramparts. At ruins ahead turn left down slope to crossing path. It is well–worth climbing mound ahead on which the Keep stood when the castle was completed in 1071. Built by Robert D'Oyley, on orders from William the Conqueror, it stood until 1652 when Cromwell ordered its destruction.

Return to crossing path, turn left and leave grounds through green gate to follow drive until, just before Town Arms, turn left to join Thames Path. Follow river bank to Benson Lock wondering, perchance, has the Victorian iron fence sunk or has the ground risen around it? At time of writing this latter section is still under negotiation for dedication as part of the National Trail – the towpath having been washed away years ago! Follow Thames Path sign over gates, then zig–zag weir and modern footbridge with view to right of former mill at Preston Crowmarsh.

Turn right along road and shortly left into path beside former 'Swan' inn. With care cross main road (A4074) and go straight on, with RAF Benson, home of 33 Squadron (Puma helicopters), away to right. Cross minor roads to emerge in village street (once the main London–Oxford road) facing pink cottage. Here go left to Crown Square. To left of the Crown lies the centre of Benson with its splendid Georgian buildings, but our way turns right, up aptly named Brook Street, complete with ducks. Soon turn left beside stone built No. 65. Behind bungalow on left notice 'Ned's Cycle Collection'. (Over 600 bikes, made between 1818 and 1930, may be viewed Easter until September by ringing Ned Passey on 01491 838414.)

Path runs behind gardens. At road go right for 25 yards then across field to join tarmac path bearing right, leading to hamlet of Rokemarsh. Here cross road onto gravel drive fronting properties, soon becoming headland path. Cross stile into meadow and shortly turn left out of field and along lane. At junction go left a few paces before entering footpath on right, soon hedged – mind the ditch! At far end turn left, along lane through Berrick Salome, bearing right at Parsonage Farm.

Take path by phone box outside Old Post Office, leading over meadow to quaint cottage style St Helen's church, still with original minstrels gallery and list of incumbents since 1087. Walk down lane to 'Chequers' and cross into gravelled Green Lane. After houses go through bridle–gate and slightly left over meadow to tall iron gate in far boundary. Here turn right on diverted path round two sides of field to leave it over wooden bridge (Ladybrook Copse). A second bridge carries bridleway on to tree lined track, becoming wide green lane, finally alongside spacious Green at Warborough.

At corner go left, signed 'Green North'. Beyond bend either take tiny path ahead to Church or continue on roadway to heart of village, opposite 'Six Bells'. If you can tear yourself away, cross main road (A329) in front of church and turn right along footway past 'Cricketers' until, facing Hall, bear left into Hammer

St Helen's Church

Lane. Where this swings right, go straight on along hedged track (Priests' Moor Lane).

At path T–junction turn left (beside the Thame), to pass under bypass to hamlet of Overy. We turn right here but do first view front of 18th century Overy Manor ahead. Now follow lane becoming path in front of Overy Mill. Raised path crosses Hurst Water Meadow (an 18 acre newly created public open space) with Dorchester Abbey visible through trees. After short length of track turn left, becoming roadway. At tree–shaded green keep left beside wall fronting houses, becoming wide gravel path leading to the massive Abbey. Turn right at Monastery Guest House, then left after lych gate to bus stop ahead.

DATE WALKED | | 19

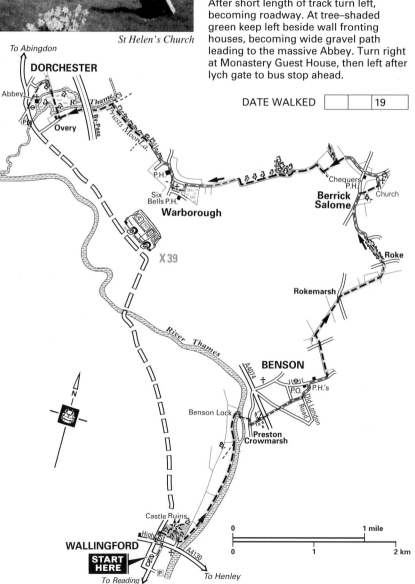

Didcot to Appleford

MAKE IT A GREAT (RAILWAY) DAY OUT!

This short walk can be combined with a visit to the Didcot Railway Centre, or the Pendon Museum in attractive Long Wittenham. Either way, allow at least an hour or two for the diversion.

DIDCOT RAILWAY CENTRE – Beside the main line station the spirit of Brunel's Great Western Railway lives on. Recapture the thrill of that era on the special Steamdays. Open every weekend. For details of the Steamdays ring: 01235 871200.

PENDON MUSEUM – A uniquely fascinating exhibition capturing in miniature the traditional beauty of the English countryside and transport around 1930. Conceived by an Australian, Roye England, work started on the project in 1931 and continues to this day. Worth walking a long way to see!
OPEN: Saturdays/Sundays (excluding December) 2–5 pm. Bank holidays from 11 am. Tel: 01865 407 365.

Distance: 4¼ miles
OS Map: Pathfinder 1136 Abingdon
START: Didcot Station
FINISH: Appleford Halt

From station forecourt turn left along footway (Station Rd). Take first turning left to pass under railway line and then immediately left again, into fenced track. At time of writing this becomes a rough path but when development is complete it will be surfaced and lit. Ignore footbridge over railway and shortly follow path ahead through subway alongside stream, under road (A4130).

Now the scenery changes dramatically! A pretty stream to follow (Moor Ditch) beside well cultivated fields. Cross road (beside Bow Bridge) and go on, with view half–right to Wittenham Clumps and half left, across brook, to spire of Appleford church. Our way parts from Moor Ditch at culvert, soon becoming hedged track. At end of field on left, headland path offers short–cut to Appleford. But we continue on track ahead, passing small playground (on right) and becoming a surfaced lane straight into Long Wittenham, a place of many varied delights, including Pendon Museum shortly on left, a Post Office cum village store and two pubs.

Joining the main street (by the one–time market cross), we suggest a gentle perambulation to the church and back. So, continue on footway past the

Old course of the Thames near Long Wittenham

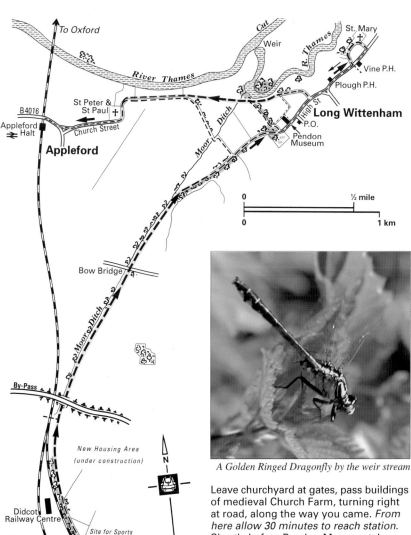

To Oxford

River Thames

Cut

Weir

R. Thames

St. Mary

Vine P.H.

Plough P.H.

B4016

St Peter & St Paul

Appleford Halt

Church Street

Appleford

High St

Long Wittenham

P.O.

Pendon Museum

Moor Ditch

Bow Bridge

Moor Ditch

| 0 | | ½ mile |
| 0 | | 1 km |

By-Pass

A Golden Ringed Dragonfly by the weir stream

New Housing Area (under construction)

N

Didcot Railway Centre

Site for Sports Ground

To Swindon

Sta.

Cow Lane

Station Road

START HERE

To Reading

Leave churchyard at gates, pass buildings of medieval Church Farm, turning right at road, along the way you came. *From here allow 30 minutes to reach station.* Shortly before Pendon Museum take footpath to right of 15 High St, gravel at first, then field–edge beside the old course of Father Thames, now the weir stream towards Clifton Lock.

Cross concrete bridge and bear right to a stepped wooden one. Go ahead and in front of large oak tree on bank, the definitive path bears right. Keeping bank with tall hedge on left, pass through two Thames–side fields. Join bridleway on left, past St Peter & St Paul and a mixed bunch of houses (in Church St.) leading into the diminutive village of Appleford. Keep right of Village Green; road ahead leads to bridge and station.

'Plough' and soon turn left beside school. At gate by 'Stables' cottage bear right on grassy path to the Norman church of St Mary. The church contains a very rare 800 year old lead font. In the south transept is the smallest sculptured monument in England, a tiny stone figure of a knight, more than 700 years old.

DATE WALKED | | 19

Clifton Hampden to Shillingford

Since Edmund Spenser wrote in 1596: 'Sweet Thames, run softly, until I end my Song', writers and poets have found inspiration by this river. As you stroll along its peaceful banks, past the one–time home of poet John Masefield, perhaps you too will feel a 'song coming on'!

Distance: 5¼ miles
OS Map: Pathfinder 1136 Abingdon
START: Bus stop at Clifton Hampden near 'Plough'. Grid ref: 548956
FINISH: Bus stop on A423 at Shillingford. Grid ref: 595929

From bus stop walk along footway, turn right at traffic lights and cross road towards Post Office store. To left of shop take gravel path, soon with steps, to lych–gate into churchyard overlooking the bridge designed by Sir George Gilbert Scott, opened in 1867 replacing a ferry.

Go past church (restored by Gilbert Scott) and down steps from south door. At foot, immediately turn left (but note here a board walk which carries roadside footway in times of flood). Our path goes under bridge, turns right up shoulder and over river. (Shortly ahead is a public car park and the 'Barley Mow', one of the prettiest Thames pubs. Built in 1350, restored after a fire in 1975, its popularity helped along by 'Three Men in a Boat'.)

However, we cross road *directly after bridge* to join Thames Path signed 'Day's Lock'. As you saunter through meadows think of London's Lord Mayor, returning from a visit to Oxford in 1826. The City Barge went aground here "for a considerable time" on the hard sandstone bottom, much to the amusement of the local peasantry!

Our way beside the Thames, sometimes called Isis here, scribes an almost symmetrical arc. The few houses of Burcot, largely hidden by trees, are on the opposite bank. The Poet Laureate, John Masefield, lived at 'Burcot Brook' on the riverside here for 30 years until his death in 1967. In 1971 the house was accidentally destroyed by fire while being converted to a Cheshire Home.

Away to our right the beech–clumps of Wittenham on the Sinodun Hills draw steadily closer until we reach and cross the weir and upper gates at Day's Lock. Stay on riverbank to recross river and go up the lane to St Peters Church, Little Wittenham. Opposite church turn left at stileway and fork left, signed Shillingford Bridge. A worthwhile detour is possible here to top of Round Hill (also visited on Ramble 20).

Our path climbs to follow clear strip through nature reserve in Little Wittenham Wood. On far side continue along broad headland, passing site of Longhill Farm. Soon after attractive house of North Farm, be careful to leave

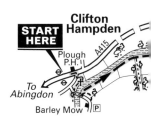

farm drive, by bearing slightly left through green gate and along delightful old hedged lane. When within sight of river ahead, turn right through another green gate, as bridleway rises through clump of mature trees and along bottom edge of field before turning up to swing–gate. Turn left to Shillingford Bridge and hotel. *From here allow 20 minutes to reach end of walk.*

Cross this handsome semi–circular arched bridge (built 1827) and take first turning left, a right–of–way carrying Thames Path. At white gate to property ahead, fork right into narrow path passing entrance to Shillingford Court. At end of wall, turn left past barrier down to river. Contemplate this pretty spot, one–time brewery wharf while relaxing, perhaps, on Alby's bench. Do notice the high water recorded here back to 1809 before strolling up this blissful street. Have you ever seen a longer wisteria than on the cottage of that name? At main road (A423) turn left to bus stop.

The frozen river at Clifton Hampden, January 1997

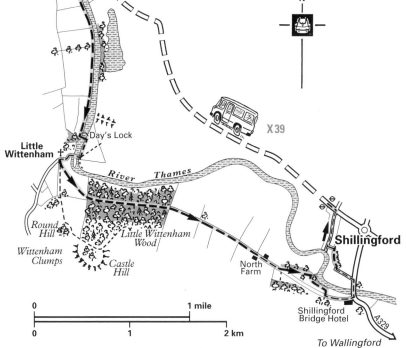

Burcot

Northfield Farm

N

Little Wittenham

Day's Lock

River Thames

X 39

Round Hill

Wittenham Clumps

Castle Hill

Little Wittenham Wood

North Farm

Shillingford

Shillingford Bridge Hotel

A329

To Wallingford

0		1 mile
0	1	2 km

Clifton Hampden to Abingdon Ramble 24

Just when it seems that the Thames Path can be just a touch tame at times, you suddenly stumble across a fascinating village, a Royal manor straight out of Domesday, set by shady pools and swirling waters. Where? Come with us....

Distance: 6½ miles
OS Map: Pathfinder 1136 Abingdon
START: Bus stop in Clifton Hampden, near 'Plough'. Grid ref: 548956
FINISH: Bus stop in Bridge Street, Abingdon

Photo: R. B. Duckett

Kingfisher

From bus stop walk along to traffic lights and turn right down towards river. The Victorian architect, Sir George Gilbert

Scott, is responsible for much we see here today; he designed the pretty (but narrow!) bridge, the church and neighbouring rectory on the bluff.

However, our route does not cross the bridge but goes straight on along the lane, past a wonderful collection of antique properties. Where road turns right, keep straight on along farm drive and ahead again at crossing track.
* Where row of trees finishes, track turns half left. Follow this between open fields to the river. This is one end of Clifton Cut which by–passes a loop of the old river through Long Wittenham.

Turn right along the riverbank of the Thames (or Isis) for a two mile stretch of restful scenery with but one interruption, the formidable Appleford railway bridge, built 1929. The next bridge we come to is at Culham, marking one end of Culham Cut, just downstream from the lock. Turn left over bridge and follow road (on a causeway) to nearby Sutton Bridge. Just beyond this bridge, by some cottages, cross road and go through swing–gate, turning left along bank of the 'old' river. Cross stile at end of field and follow track to road in Sutton Courtenay.

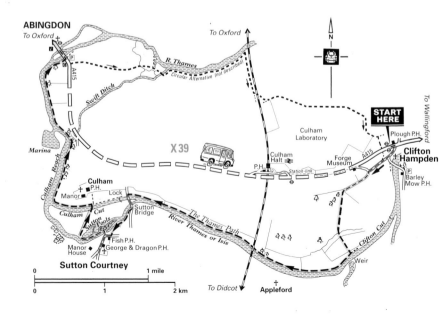